The Sharp Family, Johann Zoffany, 1779. The painting is preserved in the National Portrait Gallery, and six of the instruments, the two horns by John Christopher Hofmaster, the two clarinets by George Miller, and the two one-hand flageolets by John Mason, in the Bate Collection of Historical Instruments, Oxford. All are lent by kind permission of C. M. G. Lloyd-Baker Esq.

THE FRENCH HORN

Jeremy Montagu

Shire Publications Ltd

CONTENTS

How horns work	3
Hunting horns	6
The hand horn	12
Valve horns	19
How horns are made	29
Repertoire for the horn	30
Further reading	31
Places to visit	31

Copyright © 1990 by Jeremy Montagu. First published 1990. Shire Album 254. ISBN 0 7478 0086 3.
All rights reserved. No part of this publication may be reproduced or transmitted in any form or by any means, electronic or mechanical, including photocopy, recording, or any information storage and retrieval system, without permission in writing from the publishers, Shire Publications Ltd, Cromwell House, Church Street, Princes Risborough, Buckinghamshire HP17 9AJ, UK.

Printed in Great Britain by C. I. Thomas & Sons (Haverfordwest) Ltd, Press Buildings, Merlins Bridge, Haverfordwest, Dyfed SA61 1XF.

British Library Cataloguing in Publication Data: Montagu, Jeremy. The French horn. 1. French horns & French horn music, history. I. Title. 788.94. ISBN 0-7478-0086-3.

ACKNOWLEDGEMENTS
The author wishes to thank the Bate Collection of Historical Instruments, Faculty of Music, University of Oxford, for permission to use photographs of many French horns, most of which came from Reginald Morley-Pegge's collection. He is grateful also to Messrs Paxman of London for allowing him to photograph some of their instruments, and to the British Library for the Bull trade card. The frontispeiece, which hangs in the National Portrait Gallery, London, is reproduced by kind permission of C. M. G. Lloyd-Baker Esq. Additional photographs are by Michael Bass.

Cover: *Jonathan Williams playing a hand horn with a painted bell by Courtois neveu aîné, Paris, c.1820. (Bate Collection 6.)*

A variety of horn mutes. From left to right: fibre, metal transposing, normal metal (the Keat patent Re-ec-co-ne-mu-te). (Bate Collection 670-672.)

Jonathan Williams playing a French horn (corno da caccia) by Christian Bennett, London, c.1700. (Bate Collection 603.)

HOW HORNS WORK

Those who seek full scientific details of the acoustics of modern orchestral instruments should consult Arthur Benade's book (see 'Further reading'). This chapter explains, simply and non-technically, how horns work.

They are played by buzzing one's lips at a mouthpiece at the narrower end of a conoidal tube. If the pitch produced by buzzing the lips coincides with one of the resonant frequencies of the air column within the tube, it will resonate and produce a note. An air column will resonate not only its fundamental pitch but also a series of harmonics above that pitch.

The number of harmonics that can be obtained depends on the player's skill and on the length of the horn. The longer the horn, the easier it is to play higher harmonics, so that it takes approximately the same skill to play the 12th harmonic on the 12 foot (365 cm) narrow-bore French horn in F as the 6th harmonic on the 4 foot 6 inch (140 cm) wide-bore bugle. The player selects the different harmonics by varying the buzzing rate of the lips, aided by altering the size and shape of the mouth cavity. This procedure almost defies analysis, but it becomes instinctive with practice; the player does not have to know how it works, only that it does work. (See diagram on page 15.)

The basic pitch of the instrument, the fundamental, is controlled by the length of the tube. There is some slight variation depending on the shape of the cone, because the sounding length is that of the complete cone, whereas the actual length of the instrument is truncated because it is cut off at the mouthpiece. The cone completes itself inside the player's body when it is blown, and this extra length will vary from one instrument to

Jonathan Williams showing the hand position on a hand horn by Courtois neveu aîné, Paris, c.1820. (Bate Collection 65.)

the next according to shape. Although up to the beginning of the twentieth century orchestral horns were conical in bore save for the tuning slides, whereas today the horn has a greater proportion of cylindrical tubing than conical, this has made little difference to the physical length and only slightly more to the sound. The sound is thicker and duller than it was, but nevertheless the tone quality retains something of its original warmth and softness.

There are four ways of altering the pitch produced by a horn: altering the length of the air column, altering the area of the opening at the far end of the tube, slightly changing the tension of the lips, and sheer fakery. The last allows players to sound notes which do not exist in theory, the so-called factitious notes. These include the 1½ harmonic, written as the G between the 1st and 2nd harmonics, and the 2½, the E between the 2nd and 3rd, both of which can be played quite easily on the hand horn but only with difficulty, if at all, on the wider-bored valve horn. Skilled players could also produce other notes in the lower part of the compass, as Haydn knew, for he often wrote them, for example in the slow movement of *Symphony no 51*. Another example of factitious notes is horn-chords; the player plays one note, hums another, and, if both are in the correct relationship, a third (the resultant) appears from nowhere. The best known example today comes in Weber's *Concertino for Horn* and another is in Ethel Smythe's *Concerto for Violin and Horn*.

Altering the lip tension allows players to tune notes which are slightly out.

Altering the area of the opening allowed the hand-horn player to produce non-harmonic notes; the more the bell is stopped, the lower is the pitch produced.

The most common method of altering the pitch is by lengthening the air column, opening access to additional lengths of tubing with valves. The additional length must be proportionate to the main length, approximately one-fifteenth for a semitone and one-eighth for a whole tone. Thus the orchestral F horn has some 10 inches (25 cm) of auxiliary tubing for its semitone valve, about 18 inches (45 cm) for the whole-tone valve, and about 2 feet 6 inches (75 cm) for the tone-and-a-half valve, which are the three intervals usually provided by the valves today; the first valve horns had only the whole tone and the semitone. A horn in B flat alto, however, which is only 9 feet (275 cm) long, needs shorter lengths of auxiliary tubing, about 7 inches (18 cm), 10 inches (25 cm) and 21 inches (53 cm). This is why the double horn has two sets of valve loops and a triple horn needs three.

Another factor which affects the sound of the instrument is the shape of the mouthpiece. The more sharply cupped it is, the more brilliant the sound; the more conical it is, the smoother the sound. The narrower the throat of the mouthpiece, the more sharply focused the sound; the wider the throat, the mellower the sound. Tastes and fashions in instrumental sound change with different periods. It is thought that seventeenth-century horn mouthpieces were like trumpet mouthpieces, quite sharply cupped, with narrow throats. By the mid eighteenth century a smooth cone with no throat at all, merging smoothly into the bore of the horn, was customary, allowing the hand horn to produce a very smooth, mellow sound. Today, a combination of cone and cup with medium throat is usual, producing a sound somewhat harder and tubbier than that of the hand horn but still smoother and more mellow than that of other brass instruments.

As with all brass instruments, the tone and volume can be changed by using a mute, a stopper placed in the bell and almost closing it. Players also mute with the hand, closing the bell as far as possible and blowing harder. This produces a sharp, brassy sound, and the pitch jumps upwards. Nobody has yet produced a convincing explanation of why hand-stopping in the normal way for melodic purposes lowers the pitch, whereas fully stopping the bell while blowing harder raises it by an amount which is not proportional to the length of the tubing (by a semitone on the F horn and by about three-quarters of a tone on the B flat alto horn; the rise is in inverse proportion to the length). Reginald Morley-Pegge, the best of all writers on the horn, goes into considerable detail on this but is no nearer a solution than anyone else. Players simply accept that it happens and transpose down to compensate for the rise. A good example of this comes in Rimsky-Korsakov's *Caprice Espagnol*, where the horns play a short tune, first open and then stopped.

As with most instruments, many details which puzzle the acousticians are accepted as a matter of course by the players; they are a part of the nature of the instrument. This is why no book can explain all the details of an instrument and why no book can ever explain what it feels like to play it. In the study of any instrument, one needs to know the history and much else, but the knowledge acquired in this way remains only theory until one picks up a horn, puts one's lips to the mouthpiece, buzzes them and begins to produce music.

Left: *Jonathan Williams playing a horn by Goudot jeune, Paris, c.1842, with two Stölzel valves. (Bate Collection 600.)*

Right: *Jonathan Williams playing a modern single-F horn with three rotary valves by the Sächsische Musikinstrumenten Fabrik, Klingenthal.*

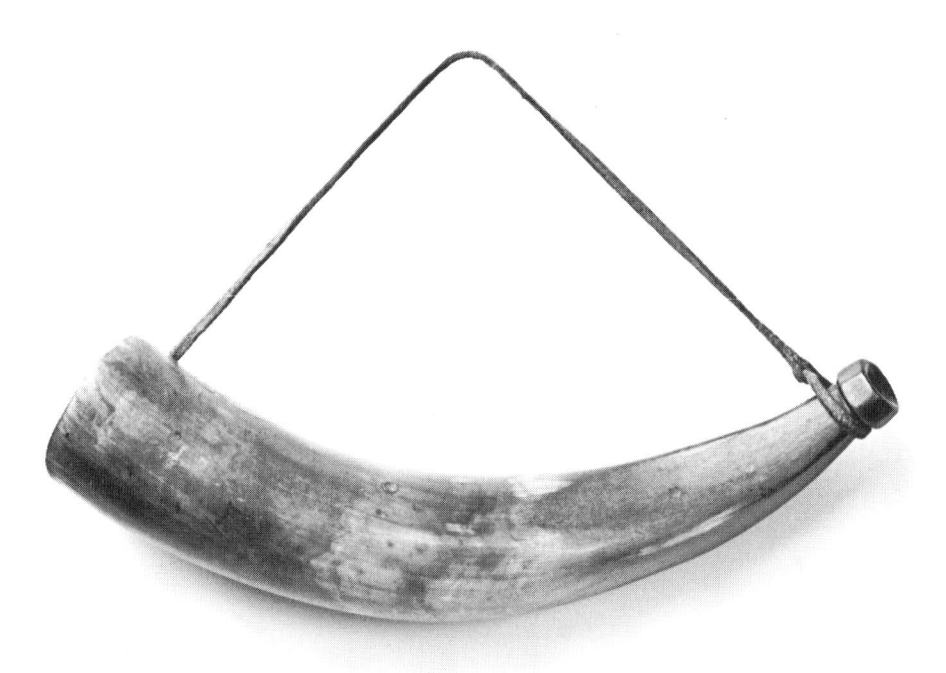

Ox horn, used in the early twentieth century by the 48th Cambridge Boy Scouts as a bugle.

HUNTING HORNS

Horns were originally made from animal horns, as the name implies. They were used for signalling and, from the middle ages onwards, for hunting calls. When the hunt became a ceremonial affair, with a number of huntsmen armed with horns, it was preferable to have horns which were long enough to play chords and fanfares together. Animal horns are too short for this, and so, in the renaissance, horns began to be made of metal.

The French horn was developed in France, as its name indicates, but it was based on two earlier instruments, at least one of which, and perhaps both, may have originated in Germany. In 1511, Sebastian Virdung, the German author of the first encyclopaedia of musical instruments, illustrated a helical horn, tightly coiled like a snail shell, which he called a *Jeger horn* (hunting horn), and an instrument of this type dating from about 1570 survives in Dresden. The other ancestor of the orchestral horn was a shorter instrument, with a single coil in its tubing. By 1636 Marin Mersenne, the great French theorist, in his famous treatise on harmony, music and instruments, wrote that the helical horn, the *cor à plusieurs tours*, was now little used and that most people used the shorter, single-coil instrument, the *trompe*. Both were hunting instruments, *cors de chasse*, and with both the huntsmen could play fanfares and chords when they gathered together to celebrate the kill at the end of the chase or to add up the score at the end of the day.

The Dresden horn is pitched in A flat, a tone below the modern bugle, and could play the same first five or six notes of the harmonic series. By the time the horn was first used in the orchestra in 1639, horns were long enough for players to sound the 12th harmonic and by 1664 the 16th, for which an instrument needs to be around 10 feet (300 cm) long, about twice the length of the Dresden

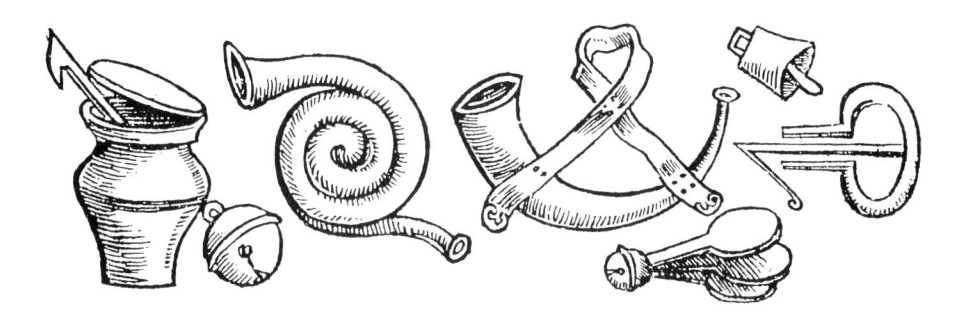

Above: *Illustration from Virdung's 'Musica Getutscht' showing a helically coiled 'Jeger horn' (hunting horn) to the left and an 'Acher horn' (watchman's horn) to the right, with a number of folk instruments.*

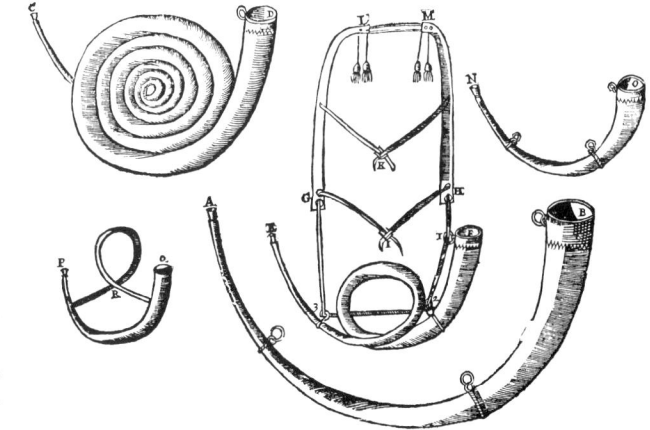

Right: *Illustration from Mersenne's 'Harmonie Universelle' showing a helically coiled horn, a trompe with a single coil with a baldric for carrying it, and three other horns.*

horn. Making an instrument of this length depended on advances in metalworking skills.

For the first century and a half, from 1511 or earlier, horns seem to have been used only in the hunting field rather than for any serious music. The reason was almost certainly the fairly raucous sound produced by the early horn. In those days, horn players did not put their hand in the bell but held the instrument with the bell upwards or outwards and blew as though they were in the hunting field. Horns were normally brought into the

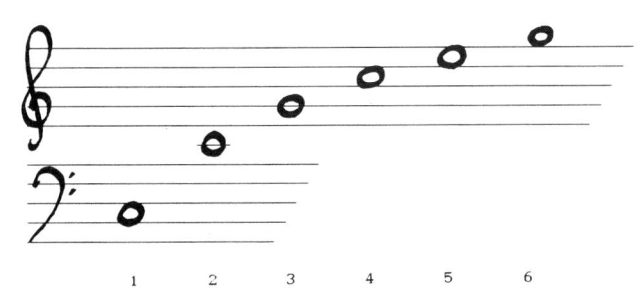

The first six notes of the harmonic series, which can be played on a horn 1 or 2 metres (3-6 feet) long, such as Mersenne's trompe or a modern bugle (in bugle notation, which reads the 2nd harmonic as middle C).

Right: *Hunting horn in D by Nicholas Winkings, London, mid eighteenth century. Winkings was French-horn maker to His Majesty's hunt. (Bate Collection 604.)*

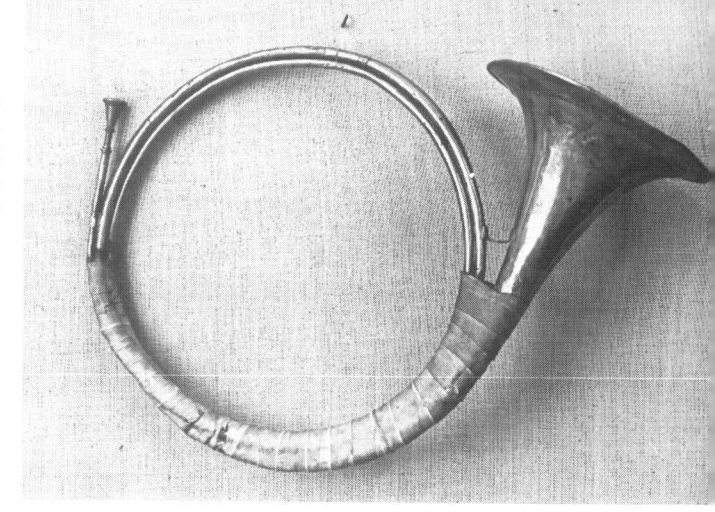

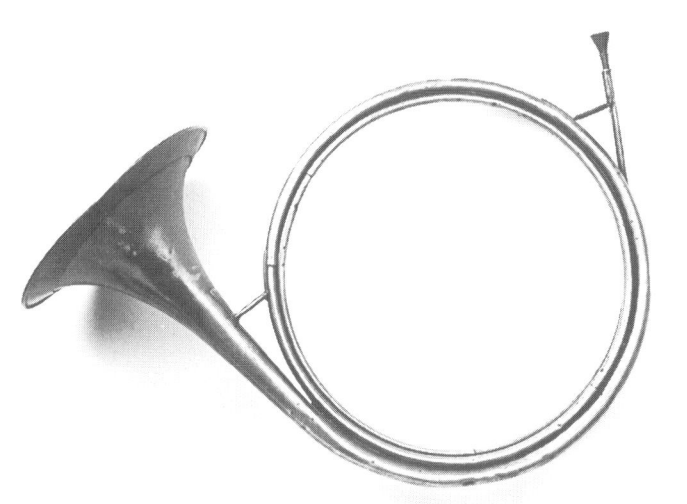

Left: *Trompe de chasse (hunting horn) in D by Carlin, Paris, mid eighteenth century. Carlin was Ordinaire du Roy. (Bate Collection 64.)*

Right: *Trompe Périnet in D by Etienne François Périnet, Paris, second quarter of the nineteenth century. The helically coiled horn, in this example with eight close coils in two parallel planes, was still being made as late as this for the French hunting field. (Bate Collection 66.)*

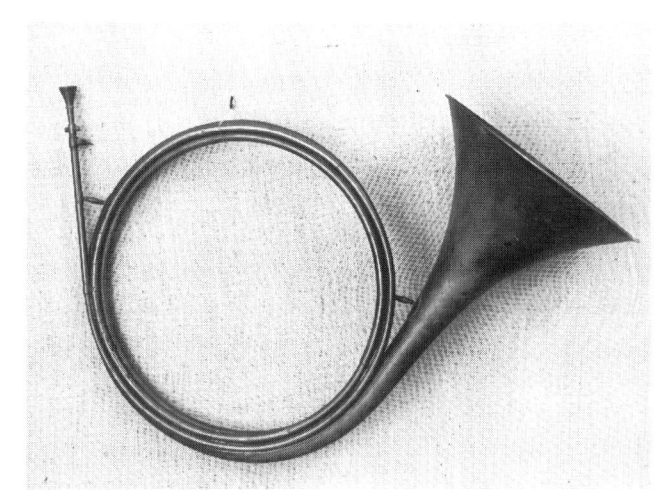

A modern trompe de chasse (hunting horn) in D by Billaudot, Paris, such as is still used by the band of the French Garde Républicaine. (Bate Collection x608.)

orchestra only for hunting scenes in operas or masques or for outdoor use such as the military band; horns of this type can still be heard in the band of the French Garde Républicaine.

In Bohemia, Austria and Germany a more refined orchestral style of horn playing began to develop. While visiting France in the early 1680s Count Franz Anton von Sporck heard the new *cor de chasse* or *parforce Horn*, a much larger instrument, with a coiled hoop big enough to pass over the huntsman's head and one shoulder. These sounded at the same pitch as the trumpets of the period, 7 feet 6 inches (225 cm) D. Count Sporck had two of his retainers taught to play these horns and took them back to Bohemia with him.

At much the same date James Talbot, an amateur scholar of music who compiled one of the few detailed accounts of instruments at that period, described much longer horns by English makers, 8-16 feet (240-480 cm) long, which sounded from C alto to C basso at what we regard as French-horn pitch today. Two such English horns survive in the key of E at modern pitch, the F of that period, and might have been used in such works

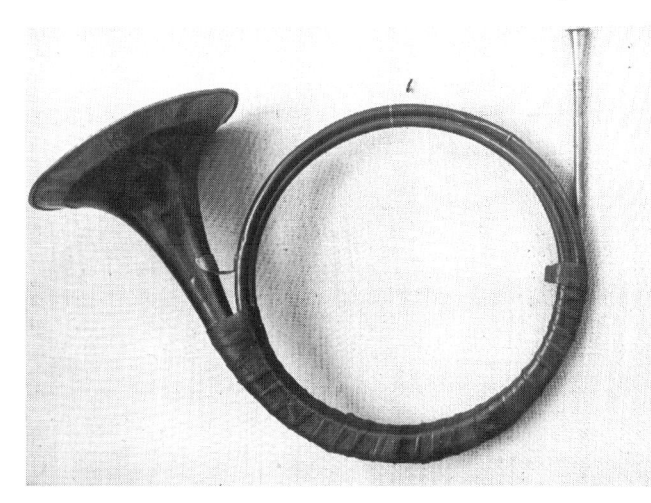

French horn by Christian Bennett, London, c.1700; in E at modern pitch (F at baroque pitch). Bennett is known only by this instrument. (Bate Collection 603.)

William Bull's trade card, c.1700, showing a 'ffrench horne' similar to that by Bennett with, to the right of its bell, an end view of the mouthpiece; the similar circle to the left of the horn is the end view of the trumpet mouthpiece. Bull was Trumpeter in Ordinary to Charles II, James II and William and Mary. His only surviving horn is in the Horniman Museum.

as Handel's *Water Music*, and it may be that French makers were also building similar instruments — William Bull, the maker of one of them, calls his a *ffrench horne* on his trade card.

The horns, called *corno da caccia* (hunting horns), for which Handel and Bach wrote their earlier parts, such as the *First Brandenburg Concerto*, were also simple instruments, coiled two or three times, depending on their length and pitch. When players wanted to use a horn in a different key, they had to use a different horn; each played in only one key, according to the length of the tubing. This was both inconvenient and expensive; to play in several keys, players had to possess several horns. A development, which almost certainly took place in Bohemia or Austria, was the introduction of the horn crook. Instead of the tubing being a continuous cone from bell to mouthpiece, the tubing was cut so that separate lengths of tubing called crooks could be inserted between the mouthpiece and the main tubing to bring the total length to that for the required pitch.

The earliest way of doing this was by a conical master crook, which accepted the mouthpiece at its narrower end, and a series of cylindrical couplers. The master

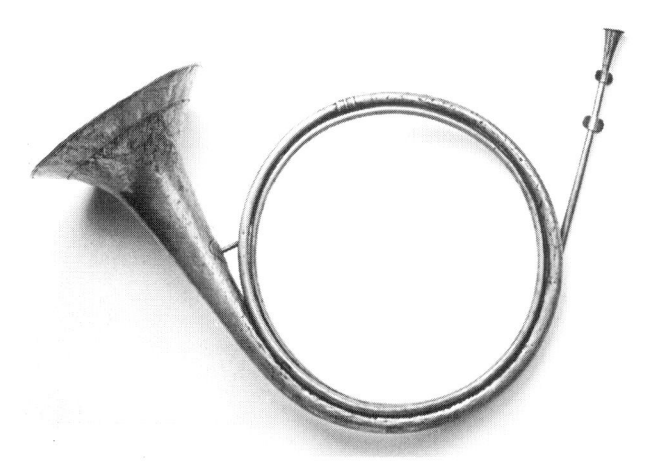

Orchestral corno da caccia in F by Ernst Johann Conrad Haas, Nuremburg, second quarter of the eighteenth century. (Bate Collection 605.)

10

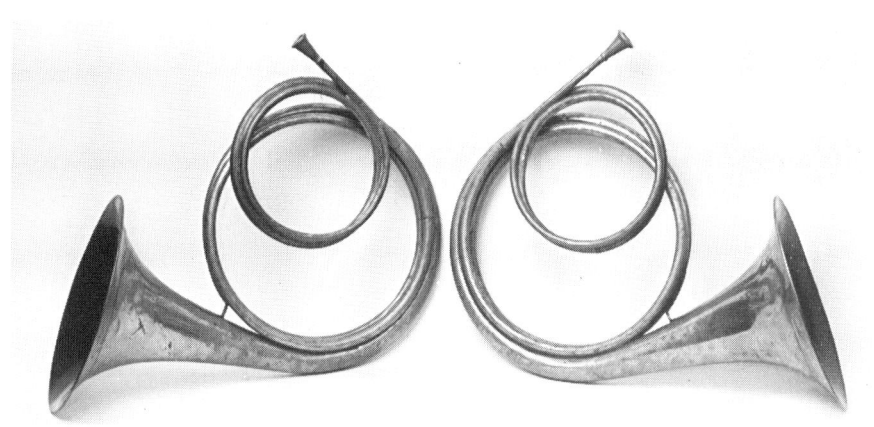

The pair of horns by John Christopher Hofmaster, London, third quarter of the eighteenth century, which are portrayed in Zoffany's well known picture of 'The Sharp Family' making music on their barge on the Thames (page 1). The pair are built left-handed and right-handed (on the right and left respectively) and are shown with their master crooks only. (Bate Collection 606 and 607; lent by C. M. G. Lloyd-Baker Esq.)

crook produced the highest key required, and the couplers, fitting between it and the body of the horn, either singly or one above the other, lengthened the tubing and brought the pitch down as far as necessary for other keys, for the longer the total length of the tubing, the lower the basic pitch.

Left: *Anonymous horn, probably Bohemian, with above it a coupler and above that a master-crook. The master crook accepts the mouthpiece and adds sufficient tubing to put the horn into the highest key in which it will be played. The coupler, placed between the crook and the instrument, adds more tubing to put the horn into any lower key required. (Bate Collection 69.)*

Right: *The same anonymous horn with the master crook and coupler in playing position.*

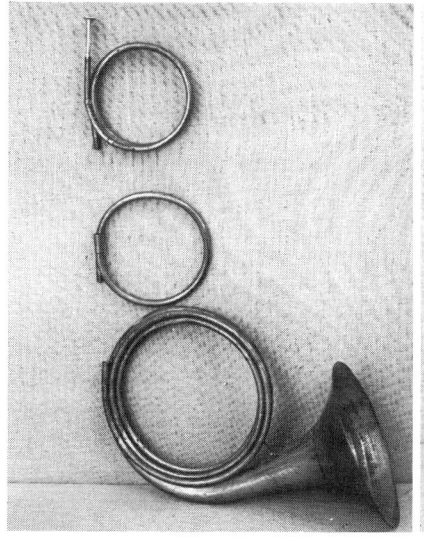

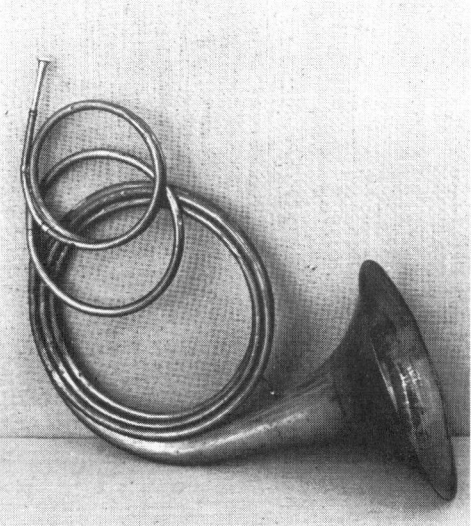

11

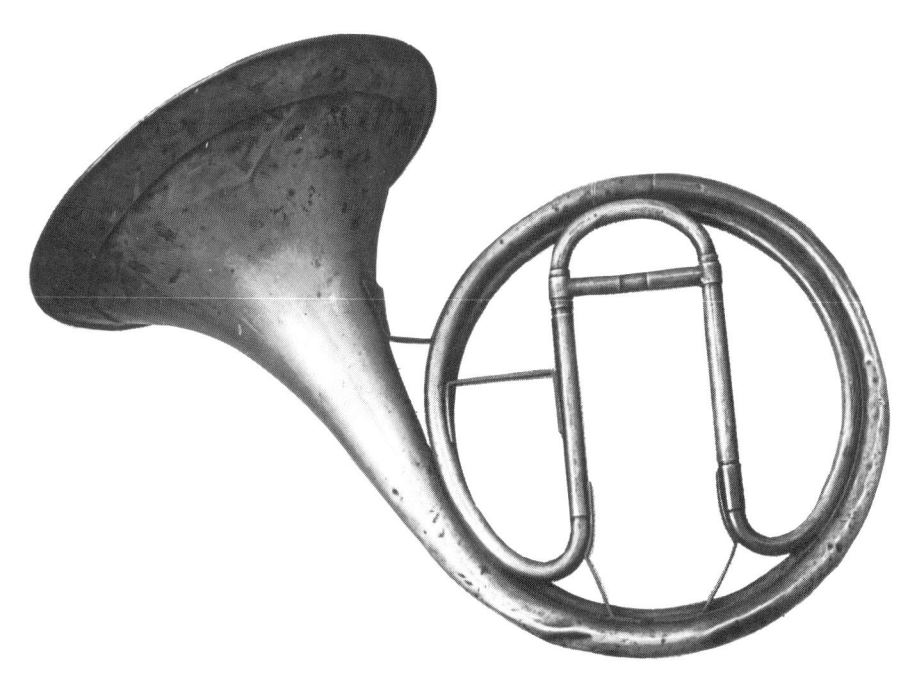

Anonymous horn, probably German, probably third quarter of the eighteenth century, with the tubing cut and bent inwards into the circle so that a tuning slide can be fitted. With later models, the legs of the tuning slide cross each other before projecting into the circle, a much stronger construction. (Bate Collection x60.)

THE HAND HORN

So long as players held their horns with the bell to the side or up in the air, the system of master crook and couplers worked well. However, when Anton Hampl, a Bohemian virtuoso at the court of Dresden, discovered that putting his hand in the bell made the sound of the horn quieter and obtained non-harmonic notes, the use of couplers became a hindrance when doing this, for it meant that the bell was at a different distance from the mouthpiece for each key. In a high key, the right arm would be cramped upwards, and in a low key the hand would have to reach down below the thigh, and therefore Hampl and the maker Johann Werner redesigned the instrument. They went back to the old idea of a fixed mouthpipe and cut the tubing nearer the centre of its length, bending the cut ends inwards into the middle of the open coil, with a U-shaped crook which slid telescopically over the two cut ends. This was possible because metalworking technology had progressed to the point where tubing could be made so exactly that such a sliding joint would move easily, when necessary, and yet stay firmly in position, without any leakage of air, when the horn was being played. By using tuning-slide crooks of different lengths, the player could put the instrument, called an *Inventionshorn*, into any key required.

The first *Inventionshorns* were built to take all sizes of crook. Around 1780 Carl Türrschmidt and the Paris maker Joseph Raoux redesigned them to take only the five crooks used by soloists, from G down to D, producing the *cor-solo*.

The majority of orchestral players had by then gone back to the use of a set of

Above left: *Horn by Smith and Sons, Wolverhampton, first quarter of the nineteenth century. This pattern, with the bell and the mouthpipe almost parallel, was surprisingly common in England even though it demands a very uncomfortable position of the right arm, with the elbow badly cramped upwards. (Bate Collection 63.)*

Above right: *Orchestral hand horn by Jean-Hilaire Asté, who took the name Halari, Paris, early nineteenth century. (Bate Collection 61.)*

terminal crooks, between the mouthpiece and the main body of the horn, each of which would accept the mouthpiece, keeping Hampl's U-shaped slide as a tuning slide; only in England and Bohemia did the use of master crooks and couplers survive into the nineteenth century. By the end of the eighteenth century there were thus two distinct types of horn: the *cor-solo*, with different lengths of tuning slide as crooks; and the orchestral horn, with a plain U-shaped tuning slide, and crooks between mouthpiece and horn.

Hampl put his hand into the bell to make a quieter sound. Horn mutes had

Below left: *Late English orchestral Inventionshorn by James Goodison, London, second quarter of the nineteenth century, shown without a crook. (Bate Collection 60.)*

Below right: *The same horn by Goodison with one of its tuning-slide crooks in position. This horn is built for a left-handed player who puts his left hand in the bell. It has a full set of crooks.*

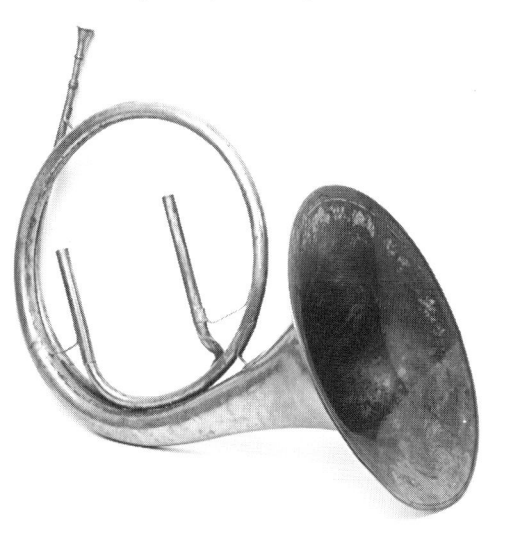

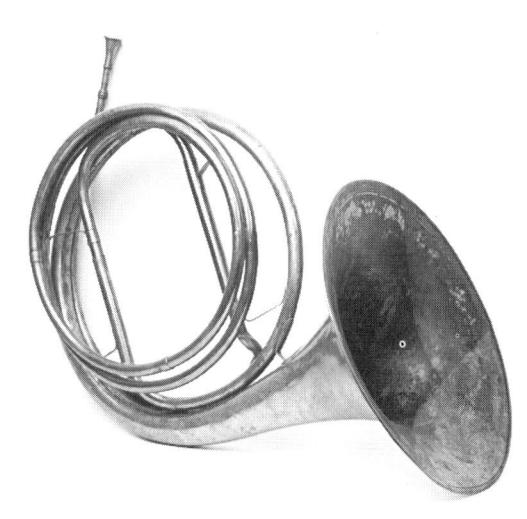

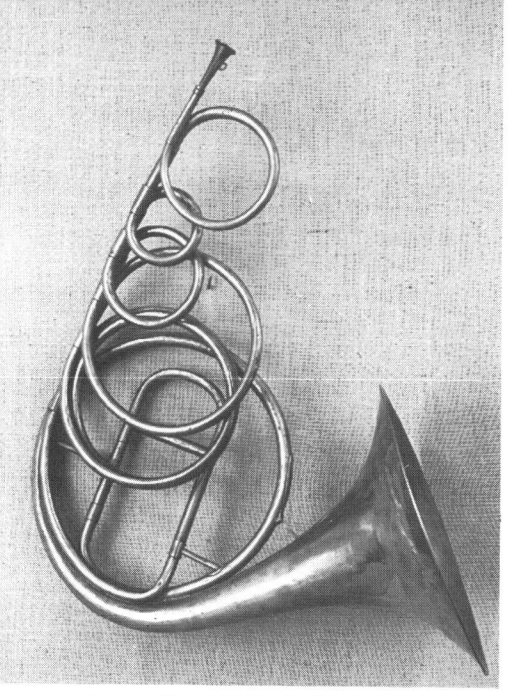

been used for some years, but it takes time to pick up a mute, put it in and take it out again, whereas the hand can be slipped in and out of the bell very quickly. When Hampl did this, he discovered that by moving his hand in the bell, obstructing it more or less, he altered the pitch. The notes that had been played on the *cor de chasse* were those of the harmonic series. These are always written in the key of C but the pitch produced varies according to the length of the instrument. A horn 12 feet (365 cm) long, the normal size today, will produce the same series of pitches, but starting on the F a fifth below the Cs in the example; a horn 9 feet (274 cm)

Left: *Horn by Thomas Key, London, early nineteenth century, with master crook and several couplers. Each coupler added moves the body of the horn further from the player's mouth and thus makes the right hand in the bell move further down. (Bate Collection 62.)*

Below: *Cor solo by Lucien-Joseph Raoux, Paris, 1823. Lucien-Joseph was the son of Joseph Raoux, who invented the cor solo. The cor solo, unlike the Goodison Inventionshorn, has crooks only for G, F, E, E flat and D (clockwise from three o'clock; the E flat crook is in the instrument), the keys in which solo works were normally written. (Bate Collection 67.)*

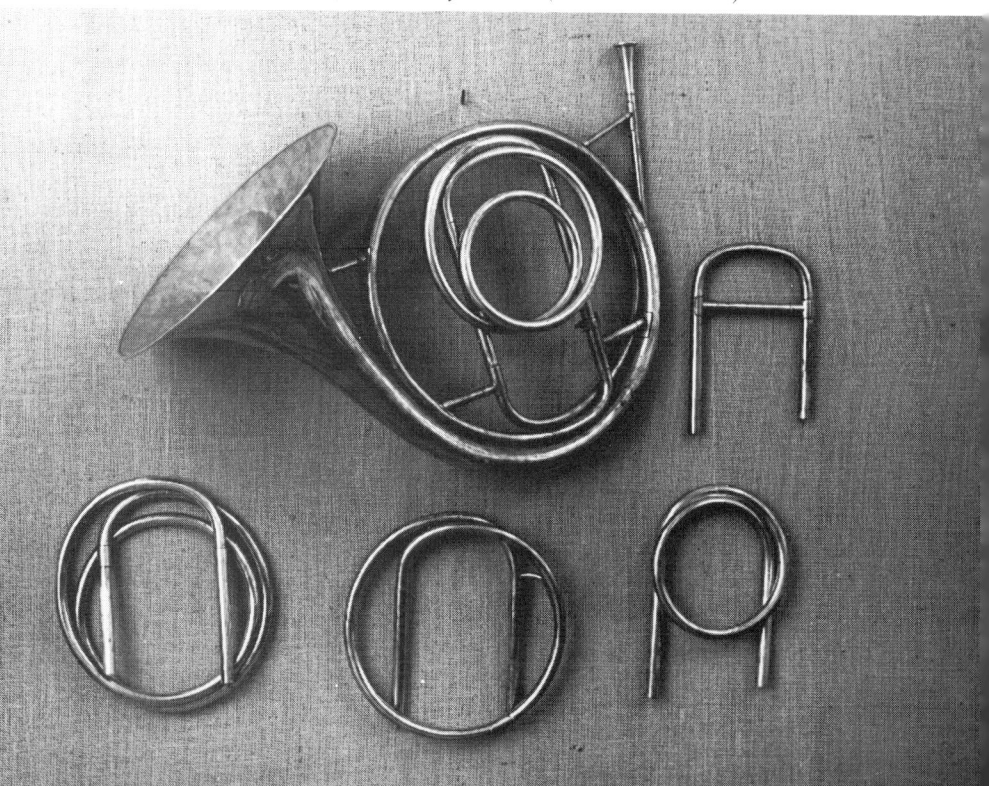

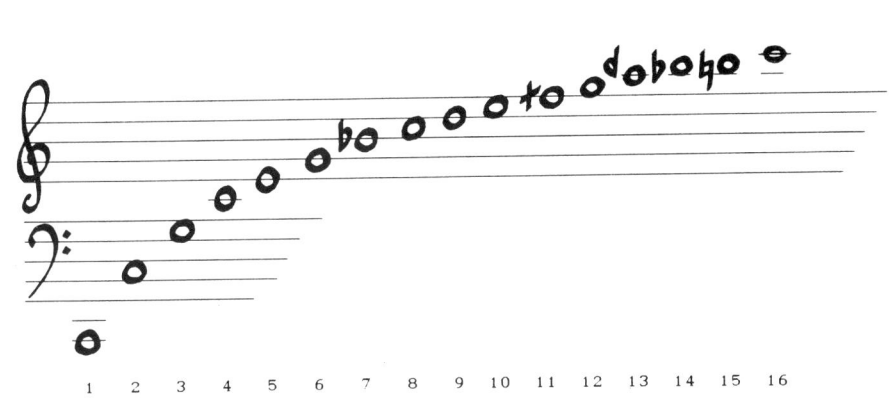

The harmonic series from the fundamental (which most players can sound only on the shorter crooks for B flat alto and A) up to the 16th ('top C'). A few composers have taken players up to the 24th, the G in alt. The series is always written on C with, for the horn, the 4th harmonic as middle C; the pitch sounded depends on the length of the horn, and on which crook is used; with the F crook, the series sounds a fifth lower than written, with the E flat a sixth lower and so forth.

long will produce the same series starting on the B flat a tone below the Cs, the pitch we call today B flat alto. Each harmonic will then be respectively a fifth or a tone lower than those written here. Harmonics are close enough together to play a melody only from the 8th harmonic upwards; this is why Bach's and Handel's parts lie so high. Hampl discovered that by moving his hand to vary the closure of the bell he could fill the gaps between the 3rd and 8th harmonics and bring into tune the very flat 7th harmonic, the 11th, halfway between F and F sharp, and the 13th, a very flat A. Previously composers had written the notes they needed, relying on players to lip the 11th down to F or up to F sharp; the writings of contemporary critics make it obvious that not all players were successful at this. With hand-stopping, it became quite easy to produce the right note.

The hand horn, as the horn played in this way was known, became a much loved instrument. It was much quieter than the *cor de chasse* and could play melodically in the lower and middle parts of the range, as we hear in Mozart's and Haydn's concertos and Beethoven's *Horn Sonata*. It was no louder than a bassoon or clarinet and Beethoven, for example, often wrote for horns and bassoons together or alternately on the same theme, as in his *Fifth Symphony* and the 'Hoffnungs Aria' in *Fidelio*. It was quiet because there is a considerable difference of tone quality between the sound of a stopped note and that of an open note, and the only way to produce an even tone quality is to stop all the notes to a lesser or greater extent. Closing the bell with the hand flattens the pitch, so players tuned the horn sharp and then flattened it a little with the hand for the 'open' notes of the harmonic series and flattened it more for the 'stopped' notes. This veiled sound, as it was called, was the ideal of all the better players, and also of composers and their audiences, and was greatly regretted when it was lost, in the middle of the nineteenth century, with the introduction of the valve horn.

The great disadvantage of the hand horn is that it cannot easily change key. It was only the soloists and the better players who could play any note required with an absolutely even tone quality, whether it was part of the harmonic series or not; the average player could tune the out-of-tune harmonics and could play an occasional non-harmonic note here and there, but little more. When the horns had to play in a new key, the player had to change crooks. This took time and might produce a clank or two as bits of tubing were taken out, put down, picked up and put in, and threw the horn out of tune because of the introduction of a length of cold tubing. Horn players had

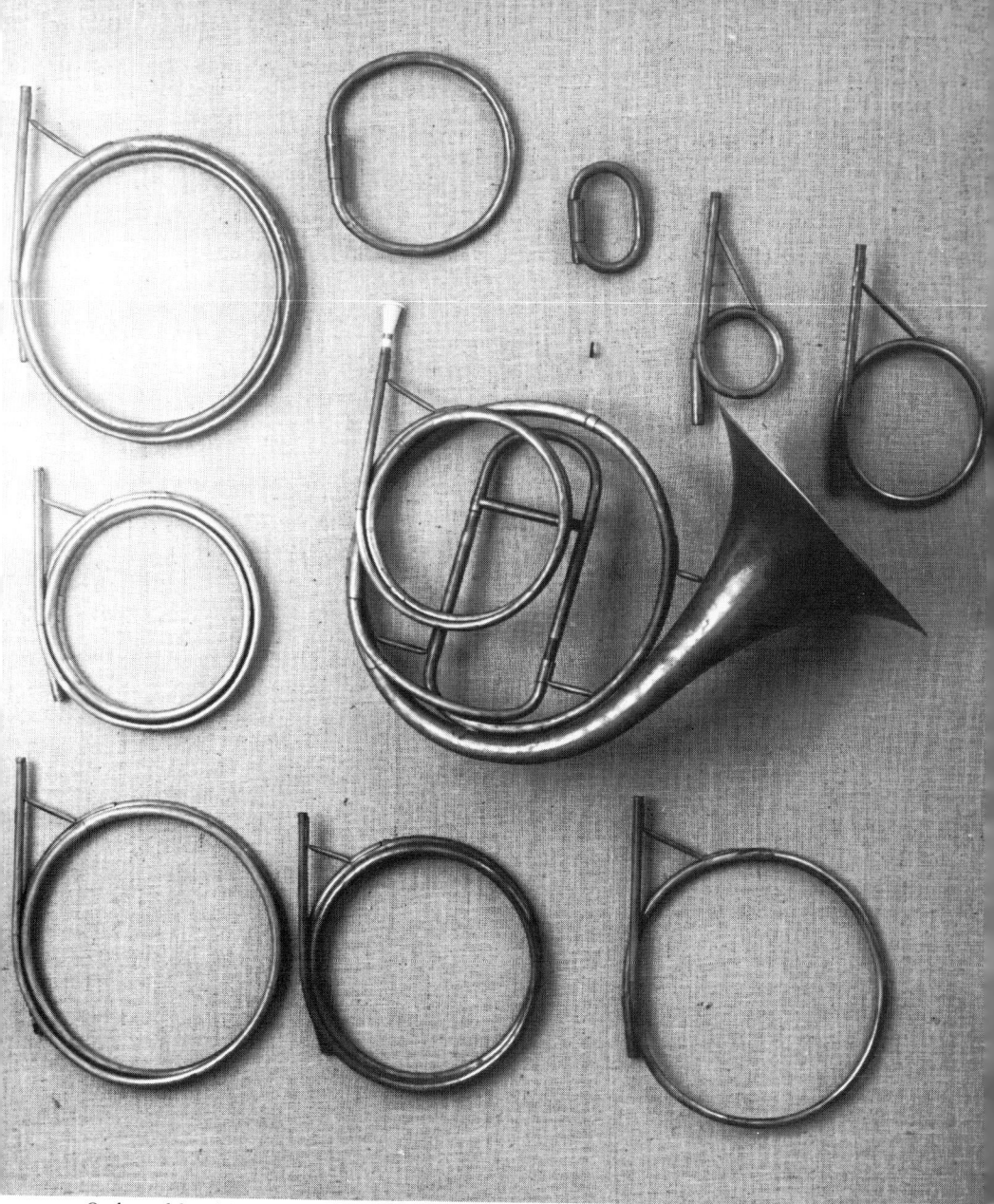

Orchestral hand horn by Courtois neveu aîné, Paris, early nineteenth century, shown with all its crooks. Anti-clockwise from top left, these are: C, D, E flat, E, G, A, B flat alto, and couplers for B natural and B flat basso; the F crook is in the instrument. French instruments never have a C alto crook, which Haydn often wrote for; only seldom does one find an A flat crook and independent B natural and B flat basso crooks. (Bate Collection 6.)

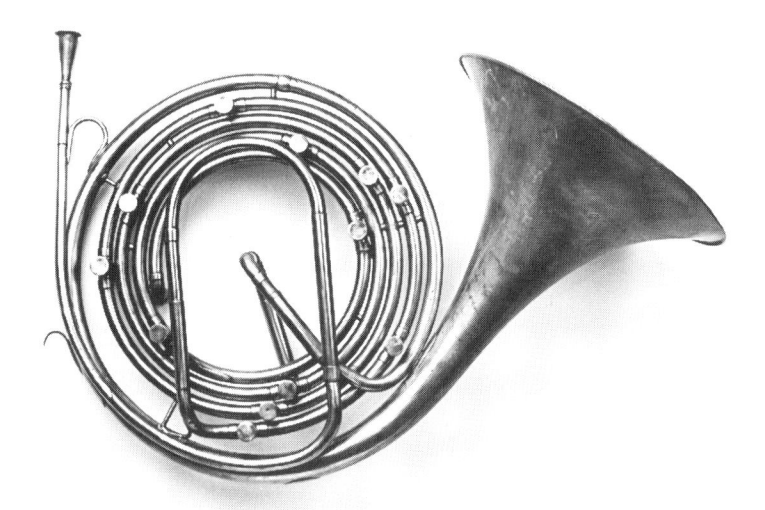

Back view of the omnitonic horn invented by John Callcott and probably made by Thomas Key. It won a prize medal at the 1851 Exhibition at the Crystal Palace, London. (Bate Collection 68.)

to carry the whole set of crooks around with them, unwieldy bundles of extra tubing. If there were a way of building crooks into the instrument, it would save much trouble and inconvenience.

One solution was the omnitonic horn. The first of these was invented in 1815, by J. B. Dupont in Paris, and the last known design was Callcott's of about 1850. The omnitonic horn has all its crooks built into it, and the player could, by shifting his mouthpiece from one tube to the next, or moving a plunger, or shifting a link-tube from one position to

The front view of the omnitonic horn shown above. The central tube is slotted into whichever socket is required and thus cuts out all the tubing further up the helix; thus the sounding length is from that point to the bell, plus the mouthpipe.

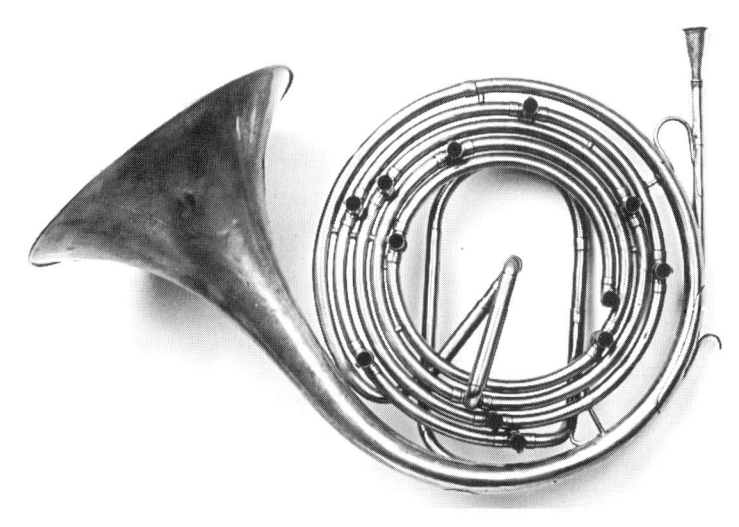

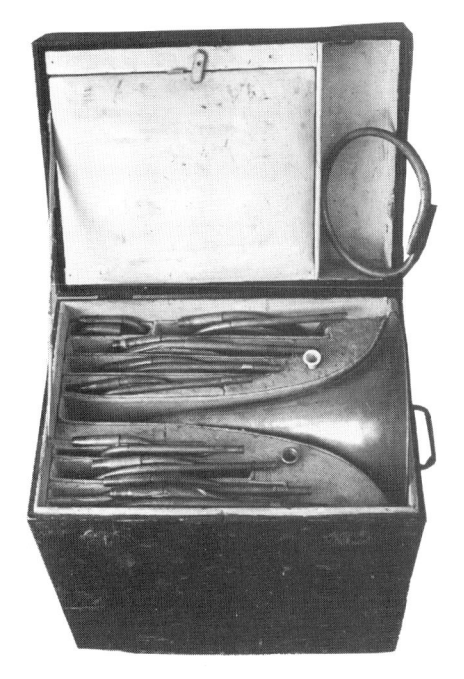

another, change from crook to crook. In each key only the harmonic series was available, and thus players still used their hand for non-harmonic notes, and the tone retained all the traditional qualities of the hand horn. The main reasons for the omnitonic horn's failure to survive were its cost and its weight, combined with its quietness due to the use of the hand, which meant that it could not compete with valve horns in the large orchestras in the new concert halls.

The final answer was also discovered in 1815. In that year Heinrich Stölzel, a German horn player, announced that he had devised a mechanism for a horn with two valves, and two years later he played such an instrument in Leipzig. The following year he and another wind player, Friedrich Blühmel, who may also have been a horn player, were granted a Prussian patent for a valve.

Left: *The Courtois hand horn (shown on page 16) in its original box with all its crooks in their slots. The box is of wood, lined with chamois leather.*

Below: *Early valve horn by Goudot jeune, Paris, second quarter of the nineteenth century, with two Stölzel valves for a semitone and a whole tone. (Bate Collection 600.)*

The horn by Thomas Key, seen earlier (page 14), with its alternative tuning slide, with two Stölzel valves, in place.

VALVE HORNS

The function of a valve is to admit or exclude the air in a length of auxiliary tubing to or from the main air column. Most piston valves have three passages or windways through them. When the valve is in its normal position, the air passes straight through one windway from the mouthpiece into the main tubing. When the valve is depressed, the entrance port to the second windway comes opposite the exit from the mouthpiece, and the air column is directed through it into the auxiliary tubing. The air passes out of the auxiliary tubing into the main tubing through the third windway. All piston valves work in this manner though differing in detail according to their type.

If the auxiliary tubing is long enough to lower the pitch of the horn by a semitone or whole tone, opening the valve has the same effect as using a crook longer to that extent, and it seems that valves and their auxiliary tubing were first thought of as a way of changing crook instantaneously. Players quickly realised that they could use the valves instead of their hands to play the notes between the harmonics. For a written C major scale in the middle register, middle C, E, G and C are already available as the 4th, 5th, 6th and 8th harmonics. A whole-tone valve provides the D and the F, the 5th and 6th harmonics of a horn a whole tone lower. A semitone valve provides the B natural, an 8th harmonic, and the whole-tone and semitone valves used together provide the A, again an 8th harmonic.

By using valves instead of the hand, players could draw their hands further out of the bell and thus play more loudly.

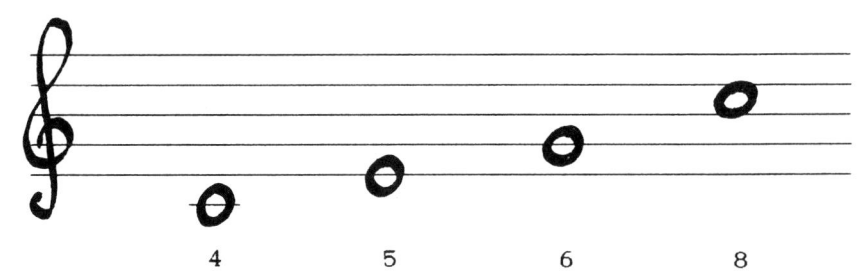

The 4th to the 8th harmonics of the open horn.

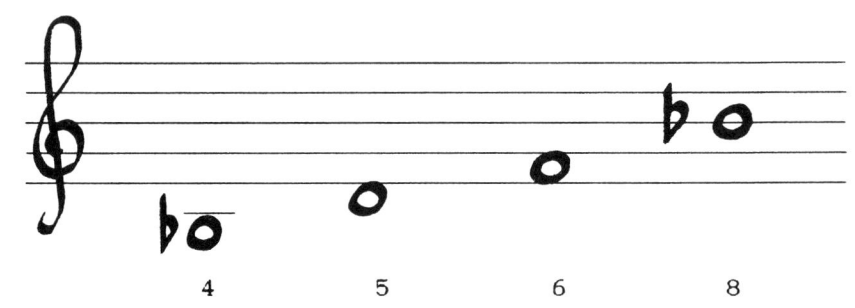

The same harmonics with the whole-tone valve operated.

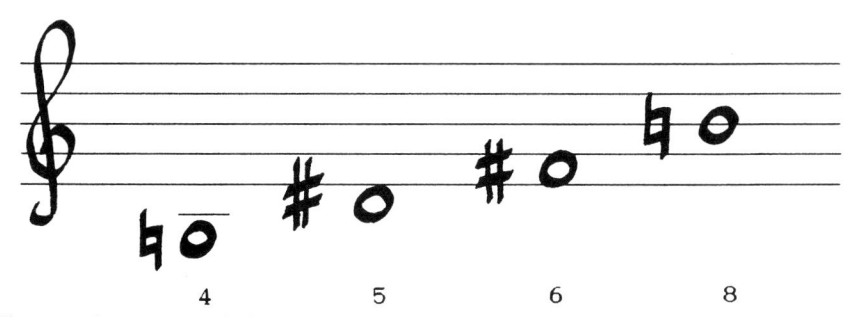

The same harmonics with the semitone valve.

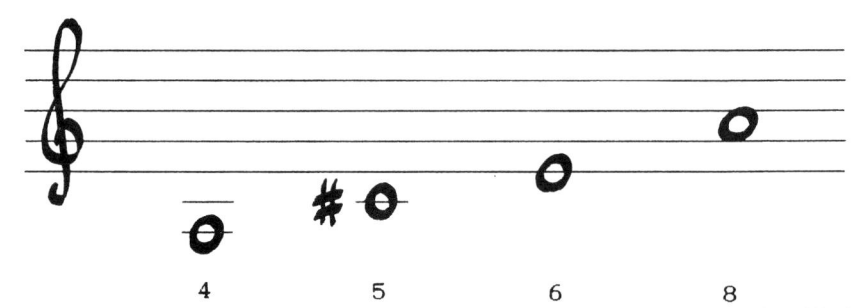

The same harmonics with both the whole-tone and semitone valves operated together. Thus the gaps between the natural harmonics in the middle of the range can be filled by using the valves.

A group of valve pistons and rotor showing the ports through which the air column is directed into the tubing. From left to right: a Stölzel piston, a Wieprecht (Berlin) piston, a Périnet piston, and a rotor from a rotary valve. These are normally invisible inside their casing.

This was becoming essential because, with the changing social conditions of the early nineteenth century, there was a demand for public concerts as well as the private concerts in the salons of the privileged and the wealthy. The costs of public concerts had to be covered by a paying audience, so that concert halls large enough to hold sufficient people were built, in which orchestras had to produce enough sound to be audible to a large audience. The string sections of the orchestra grew larger, and wind instruments had to be louder to balance them. The loss of the veiled sound of the horn was inevitable if a louder sound was required.

Many types of valve were invented dur-

Close-up view of a set of Wieprecht (Berlin) valves on an instrument. (Bate Collection 662.)

Horn by Rudall Carte, London, late nineteenth century, with three Périnet valves. (Bate Collection 628.)

ing the nineteenth century, and the best general history of the valve is that by A. C. Baines. The first valves were square in section but no horn survives with these. The five types of valve most important to the horn are: Stölzel's second design, a long-stroke narrow cylindrical piston, known today as the Stölzel valve, for it was widely used, and many instruments with that valve survive; Uhlmann's double piston of 1830, the Vienna valve; Riedl's *Radmaschine* of 1832, the rotary valve; Wieprecht's wide-bore piston of 1833, the Berlin valve; and Périnet's medium-bore piston of 1839, the Périnet valve. The two most commonly used on horns today are the rotary and the Périnet; the Périnet is now found only in France but, until the middle of the twentieth century, it was also used in Britain; the rotary is used in all other places except Vienna, where the Uhlmann double-piston valve still predominates.

Stölzel's cylindrical piston has only two passageways, one diagonally across the piston and the other leading from the open bottom of the piston to a pair of holes opposite each other in its side. The air enters or leaves the valve through the bottom of the piston and turns a right angle as it passes either into the auxiliary tubing through one of the holes, or across the link-tube through the other into or from the next valve, depending on whether the piston is up or down. The sharp 90 degree bend and the narrow tubing tended to inhibit the free vibration of the air column and led to criticism of its choked tone.

Wieprecht's piston was shorter and thicker, with three passageways. One allows the air to pass straight across the valve when it is not depressed, and the other two, side by side, deflect the air into and out of the auxiliary tubing. It was, on the whole, a more successful valve, but when makers used oval passageways to save space there was, again, some choking of the air column.

Périnet's piston, medium in diameter and length, has proved the more successful because, with the three passageways one above the other, there was less need to restrict their diameter, and because the bends were comparatively gentle curves instead of right angles.

Uhlmann's pistons are similar to the Stölzel in that the bottom of the piston

Horn by Couesnon, Paris, early twentieth century, with three Périnet valves, the third ascending (cutting out a whole-tone when operated). This system is popular in France; it leaves two notes at the very bottom of the range (low E flat and D) unobtainable except by hand-stopping, but it improves a number of notes in the middle and the top of the range. (Bate Collection 636.)

Close-up view of Vienna valves on a horn by Uhlmann.

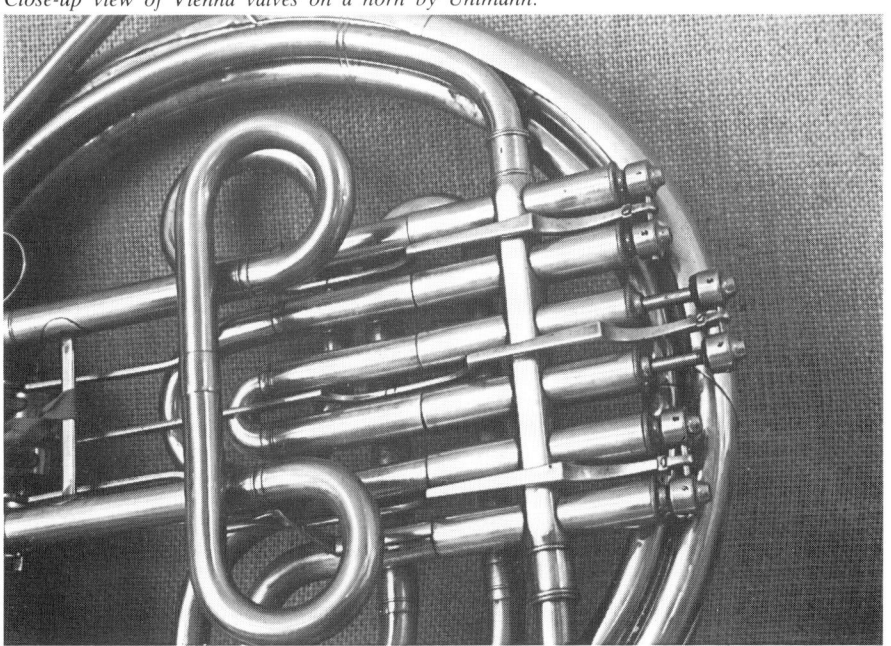

Front view of Vienna model horn in F by Leopold Uhlmann, mid nineteenth century. (Bate Collection 635.)

Back view of the same Uhlmann horn. A close-up of the valves was shown earlier.

forms part of the windway, but simpler because, since the pistons are twins, one deflects the air into the auxiliary tubing and the other deflects it out; they are therefore much shorter than the Stölzel valve. They have survived because, although the Viennese horn is more difficult to play well than either the French or the German, its beauty of tone is unsurpassed, and the Viennese orchestras have refused to abandon it, even though for a while it looked as though the German instrument would supplant it.

The German horn has for many years been built with rotary valves. These are by far the simplest and the most efficient. The rotor has two windways through it which, when it is rotated 90 degrees, deflect the air into and out of the auxiliary tubing; in the position of rest, one passes the air straight on into the main tubing.

A German horn-maker, Fritz Kruspe of Erfurt, realised that much of the difficulty in playing the horn lay in the fact that the higher harmonics are very close together. A player aiming at a 12th harmonic has to be very exact in his pitching to avoid playing an 11th or a 13th by mistake. If the tubing were shorter than the 12 feet (365 cm) of the horn in F, the usual length and key for the valve horn, he would be able to produce the same pitch as a lower harmonic of a shorter tube. Kruspe therefore added an extra valve which cut out about 3 feet (91 cm) of tubing and changed the basic pitch from F to high B flat. A double horn, as these instruments are called, has two pairs of windways through the rotors because two sets of auxiliary tubing are needed for the valves, one above the other; the auxiliary length must be proportionate to the length of the main tubing (see 'How horns work').

An anonymous Eastern European horn in F, probably late nineteenth century, with rotary valves controlled by clock springs. (Bate Collection x65.)

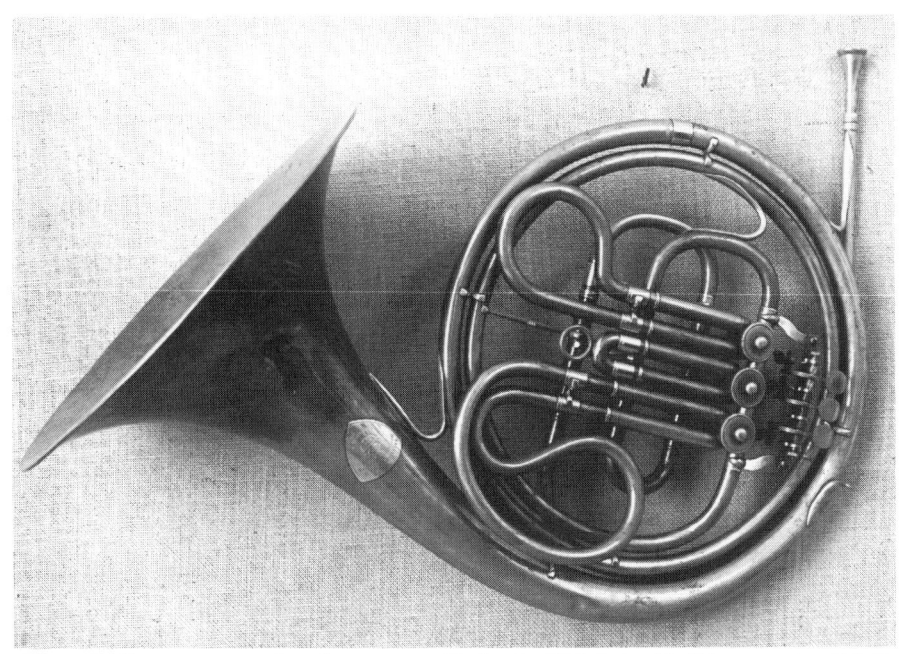

A horn in F, more recent than that on page 25, by the Sächsische Musikinstrumenten Fabrik, Klingenthal, with three rotary valves controlled by coiled wire springs. (Bate Collection x634.)

There are today two different types of double horn. The full double has auxiliary tubing sufficient both for the F and the B flat sides of the instrument. The compensating double has one set sufficient for the B flat side, and the second set is only the length of the difference between that set and what would be needed for the F side. Thus on a full double either set of auxiliary tubing is in use, but never both, whereas on the compensator the B flat set is used when playing on that side, and both sets are used when playing on the F side. As a result the compensator is much lighter in weight than the full double, but more difficult to set in tune.

Paxman of London have invented a triple horn to shorten the tube length still further, making instruments in F, high B flat and high F; the note written as a 12th harmonic can then be played as a 6th harmonic on the high F side. Players who spend much of their time on high parts have taken to even higher double horns, an octave higher than Kruspe's, in high F and highest B flat. These piccolo horns are very useful in modern professional conditions, when players hurry from rehearsals to recording sessions and back to concerts, with little leisure for practice and unremitting pressure to play the right notes every time. However, unless they are played with great care and discretion, piccolo horns can sound much like flugelhorns, which are the same length and pitch.

An instrument which was demanded by Richard Wagner for his *Ring* operas has proved successful enough to be used by many other composers, for example Bruckner in his *Seventh Symphony* and Stravinsky in *The Rite of Spring*, and it is often heard in recording studios for film and other music. This is the Wagner tuba or, as it is usually known today, the tuben. Wagner specified an instrument which would sound louder than a horn without either the tonal weight of a true tuba or the brilliance of a trumpet.

A modern full double horn in F and B flat alto by Gebrüder Alexander, Mainz.

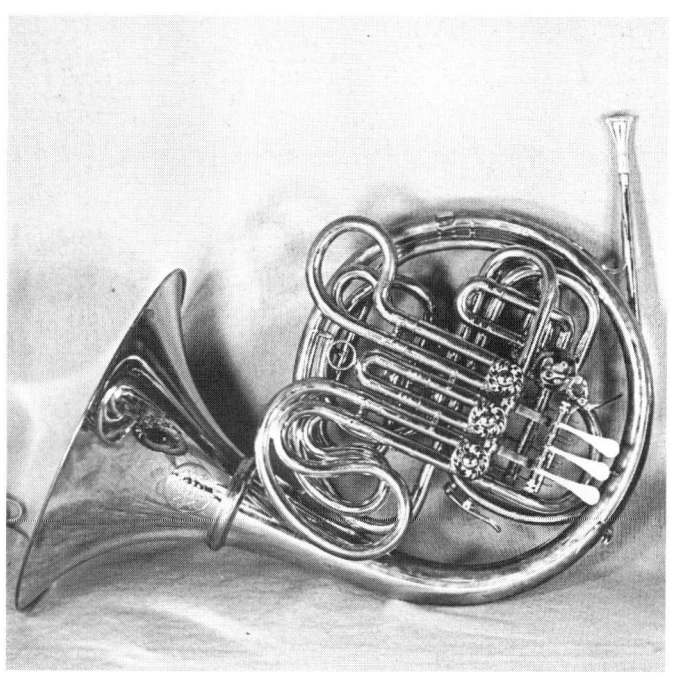

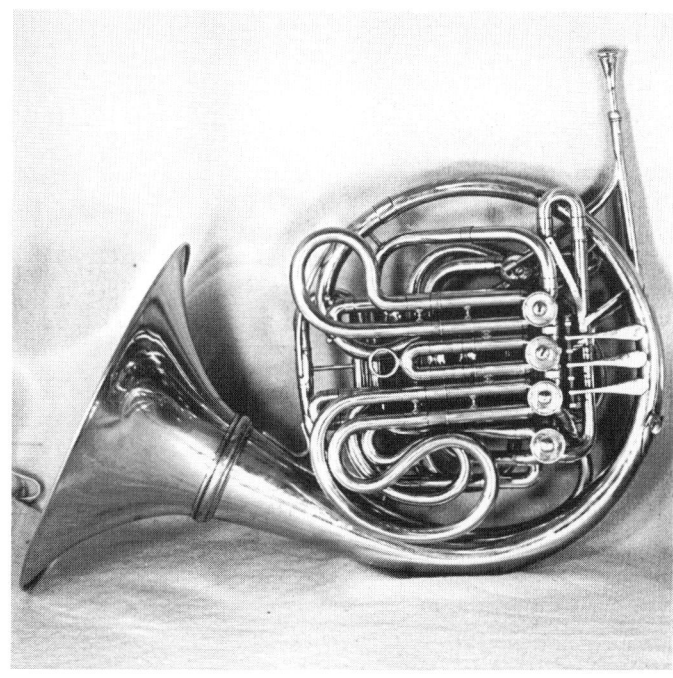

A triple horn by Paxman Brothers, London, c.1980, in F, B flat alto and F alto.

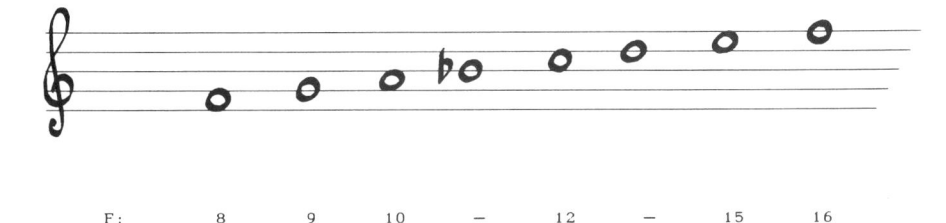

Bb alto: 6   —   —   8   9   10   —   12

F: 8   9   10   —   12   —   15   16

The harmonic series in actual pitch, from the 8th to the 16th, numbered below for the F horn, and above for the B flat alto. It can thus be seen that the pitch for which the player must produce a 16th harmonic (a top C written) on the F horn is only a 12th harmonic on the B flat alto. On the F alto it would be an 8th harmonic, and on the B flat piccolo a 6th. Note that some pitches, which are not natural harmonics on the F side, are harmonics on the B flat, and vice versa.

Baines suggests that he probably had one of Adolphe Sax's inventions in mind, but C. W. Moritz, the famous Berlin brass-instrument maker, produced the instrument which became accepted. Tubens are built in the same oval shape as the German tenor or baritone tubas, but they are nearer to horns in bore and are in the normal horn keys of F and B flat. Some makers now make tubens like double horns, in both F and B flat.

Left: *Front view of a modern double Wagner tuba in F and B flat by Paxman Brothers, London.*

Right: *Back view of the same Wagner tuba.*

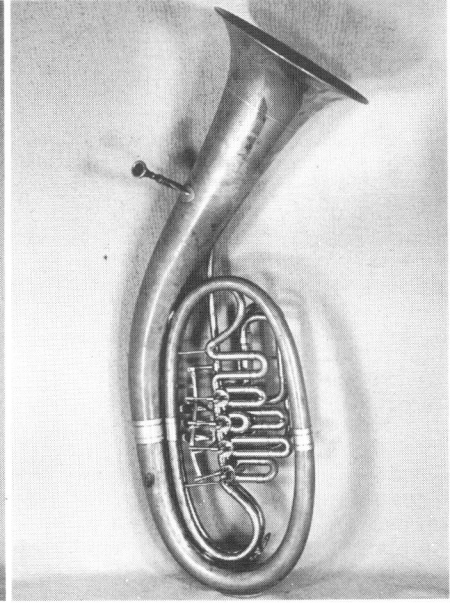

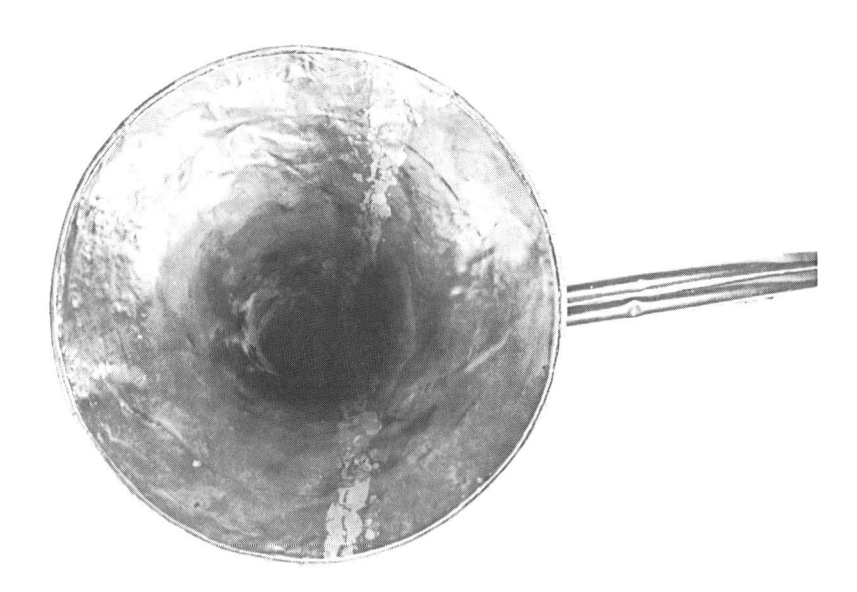

Detail of the bell of the horn by Christian Bennett seen earlier (pages 3 and 9), showing the seams of the gusset where an extra piece of metal was inserted into the bell to make the flare without thinning the main sheet of metal too much.

HOW HORNS ARE MADE

In the sixteenth and seventeenth centuries the tubing was raised from long, very narrow, triangular sheets of silver or brass, hammered round a long, tapering steel mandrel, and brazed together with a longitudinal seam. It was then driven through a hole in a lead block to smooth out any wrinkles and to force the tube to a tight fit on the mandrel. The mandrel was then removed. The tubing was filled with lead or pitch, and it was bent to the desired curve; without a filling, it would be badly wrinkled. The several sections were then soldered together, end to end, with a metal ferrule soldered over each joint to hold them securely. For the bell flare, it was necessary to insert a V-shaped gusset, which usually made up between a third and a half of the total circumference of the end of the bell. Finally the metal was scraped and planished to remove all tool marks, and a garland, a band of metal on which the maker's name could be engraved, was fitted round the end of the bell to strengthen it.

Instruments today require much less skill in their construction, but much higher technology, for brass tubing is no longer raised from sheet by hammering it by hand. Even conical-bore tubing can be drawn or extruded by machine, and the various bends and curves formed hydraulically in moulds. Bells are not gusseted but are spun from a sheet of brass, pressing the brass to a rapidly revolving steel mandrel of the required shape, and then, instead of a garland, rolling the end of the bell back over a wire ring to support it. The result is that the modern horn sounds very different from the older instrument, for the way in which the metal is treated affects the sound it produces. Because of the growing interest in recreating the sound of earlier music on reproductions of the original instruments, a few firms have returned to the older methods of manufacture for their reproductions; others are making their instruments by modern methods, so that although they may look like reproductions, they sound like modern instruments.

REPERTOIRE FOR THE HORN

FOR CORNO DA CACCIA
Bach, J. S.: *Brandenburg Concerto no. 1*, BWV 1046.
Bach, J. S.: *Mass in B minor*, BWV 232.
Bach, J. S.: orchestral parts in many cantatas.
Handel, G. F.: *The Water Music*, HWV 348 and 349.
Handel, G. F.: *Music for the Royal Fireworks*, HWV 351.

FOR HAND HORN
Beethoven, L. van: *Egmont Overture*, op. 84 (especially the coda at the end).
Beethoven, L. van: the 'Hoffnungs Aria' (also called 'Abscheulicher') from *Fidelio*, op. 72.
Beethoven, L. van: *Horn Sonata*, op. 17.
Beethoven, L. van: *Sextet* for two horns and strings, op. 81b.
Beethoven, L. van: *Symphony no. 3 'The Eroica'*, op. 55.
Beethoven, L. van: *Symphony no. 9 'The Choral'*, op. 125 especially the fourth horn solo in the slow movement.
Brahms, J.: *Horn Trio* op. 40.
Brahms, J.: *Piano Concerto no. 2* in B flat, op. 83, especially the introduction.
Brahms, J.: all his symphonies have beautiful passages for the horns.
Haydn, F. J.: the two *Horn Concertos*, Hob. VIId 3 and 4.
Haydn, F. J.: many symphonies, especially no. 31 in D (*The Horn Signal*) and 51 in B flat, with extremely high solos in the slow movement.
Mendelssohn, F.: 'Nocturne' from *The Midsummer Night's Dream*, op. 61 no. 7.
Mendelssohn, F.: *Symphony no. 4 'The Italian'*, op. 90, especially the Trio of the third movement.
Mozart, W. A.: the four *Horn Concertos*, K. 412 (K. 386b), 417, 447 and 495.
Mozart, W. A.: *Quintet for Horn and Strings*, K. 407 (K. 386c).
Rossini, G.: *Overture to Semiramide*, especially the opening.
Weber, C. M. von: *Concertino for Horn*, op. 45 (Jähns 188), especially notable for the chords for the solo horn.
Weber, C. M. von: *Overture to Oberon*, Jähns 306, especially the opening.

FOR VALVE HORN
Berlioz, H.: 'Chasse royale' from *Les Troyens*, Holoman 133A no. 29.
Britten, B.: *Serenade for Tenor, Horn and Strings*, op. 31.
Mahler, G.: *Symphony no. 5*.
Ravel, M.: *Pavane pour une Enfante défunte*.
Rimsky-Korsakov, N. A.: *Caprice Espagnol*, op. 34.
Schubert, F.: *Auf dem Strom* for voice, horn and piano, D. 943; the first work that it is certain was written for valve horn.
Schumann, R.: *Concertstück for Four Horns*, op. 86.
Strauss, R.: the two *Horn Concertos*, op. 11 and op. AV. 132.
Tchaikovsky, P. I.: *Symphony no. 5*, op. 64, especially the slow movement.
Wagner, R.: *The Ring of the Nibelung*, WWV 86.
Wagner, R.: *Siegfried Idyll*, WWV 103.
Wagner, R.: *Tannhäuser Overture*, WWV 70, which asks for two hand horns and two valve horns.

This is only a very small selection of solo and orchestral music. The horn is often the glue that sticks together the various sections of the orchestra, and it also has many delightful little solo passages. There is also a very large chamber music repertoire, mainly wind quintets today, but this includes, too, the divertimenti and serenades of the eighteenth and early nineteenth centuries, many of them written for the military band of the period: two oboes, two clarinets, two horns and two bassoons. It is only when music is performed on 'authentic' instruments that any of this repertoire is played on anything other than a modern valve horn.

FURTHER READING

Baines, Anthony. *Brass Instruments, Their History and Development.* Faber and Faber, 1976.
Baines, Anthony. 'James Talbot's manuscript', *The Galpin Society Journal*, volume 1 (1948), 9-26.
Benade, Arthur. *Fundamentals of Musical Acoustics.* Oxford University Press, 1976.
Fitzpatrick, Horace. *The Horn and Horn-Playing and the Austro-Bohemian Tradition 1680-1830.* Oxford University Press, 1970.
Mersenne, Marin. *Harmonie Universelle.* Paris, 1636. (Facsimile, Centre National de la Recherche Scientifique, Paris, 1963.)
Montagu, Jeremy. *The World of Medieval and Renaissance Musical Instruments.* David and Charles, 1976.
Montagu, Jeremy. *The World of Baroque and Classical Musical Instruments.* David and Charles, 1979.
Montagu, Jeremy. *The World of Romantic and Modern Musical Instruments.* David and Charles, 1981.
Morley-Pegge, Reginald. *The French Horn.* Ernest Benn, 1960.
Pizka, Hans. *Das Horn bei Mozart.* Hans Pizka, Kirchheim bei München, 1980.
Sadie, Stanley (editor). *The New Grove Dictionary of Musical Instruments.* Macmillan, 1984.
Talbot, James. See Baines, above.
Virdung, Sebastian. *Musica Getutscht.* Basel, 1511. (Facsimile, Bärenreiter, Kassel, 1970.)

PLACES TO VISIT

GREAT BRITAIN
The Bate Collection of Historical Instruments, Faculty of Music, St Aldate's, Oxford OX1 1DB. Telephone: 0865 276139.
Edinburgh University Collection of Historic Musical Instruments, Reid Concert Hall, Bristo Square, Edinburgh EH8 9AG. Telephone: 031-667 1011, extension 2573.
The Horniman Museum and Library, London Road, Forest Hill, London SE23 3PQ. Telephone: 081-699 2339.

AUSTRIA
Kunsthistorisches Museum (Sammlung alter Musikinstrumente), Neue Burg, A-1010 Vienna.
Salzburger Museum Carolino Augusteum, Museumsplatz 6, A-5010 Salzburg.

BELGIUM
Musée Instrumental du Conservatoire Royal de musique, Rue Montagne de la Cour, B-1000 Brussels.

FRANCE
Musée Instrumental du Conservatoire National Supérieur de Musique, 14 rue de Madrid, F-75008 Paris.

GERMANY
Bayerische Nationalmuseum, Prinzregentenstrasse 3, D-8000 Munich.
Deutsche Museum, Museuminsel 1, D-8000 Munich.
Germanisches Nationalmuseum (Sammlung historischer Musikinstrumente), Kartäusergasse 1, D-8500 Nuremburg 11.

Musikinstrumenten Museum, Staatliches Institut für Musikforschung, Preussischer Kulturbesitz, Tiergartenstrasse 1, D-1000 Berlin 30.
Musikinstrumenten-Museum der Karl-Marx-Universität, Täubchenweg 2c-e, DDR-701 Leipzig.

ITALY
Conservatorio di Musica Luigi Cherubini, Museo degli Strumenti Musicali, Piazetta della Bella Arti 2, I-50100 Florence.

NETHERLANDS
Haags Gemeentemuseum, Stadhouderslaan 41, NL-2517 HV The Hague.

UNITED STATES OF AMERICA
Metropolitan Museum of Art, Fifth Avenue at 82nd Street, New York, NY 10028.
Museum of Fine Arts, Huntington Avenue, Boston, Massachusetts 02115.
Shrine to Music Museum, 414 East Clark Street, Vermillion, South Dakota 57069.
Smithsonian Institution, National Museum of History and Technology, Division of Musical Instruments, Constitution Avenue, Washington, DC 20560.

USSR
Museum of Musical Instruments, Institute of Theatre, Music and Cinema, 5 St Isaac's Square, 190000 Leningrad.